Reflections of Huntington Beach

A photographic retrospective from Brian Barsuglia

Volume 1

A brief legend on the final page tells the story of each photograph.

REFLECTIONS OF HUNTINGTON BEACH
Copyright © 2020 by Brian Barsuglia

All photos and contents of this book are the original works of Brian Barsuglia.

All rights reserved. No part of this book may be used or reproduced in any manner whatsoever without written permission, except in the case of brief quotations embodied in critical articles or reviews.

A Koa Aloha Media Book
Published by Koa Aloha Media
ISBN: 9798601820967

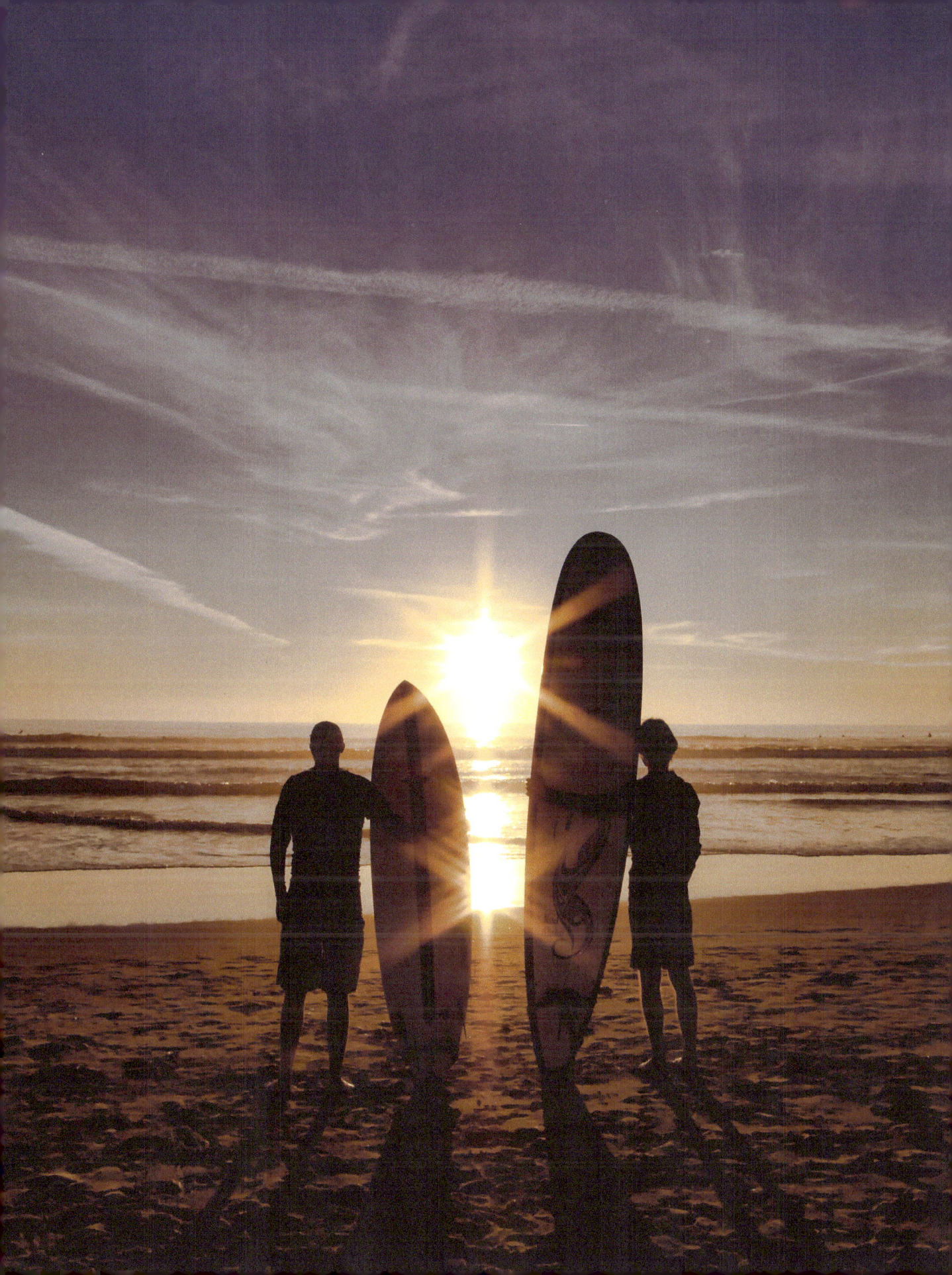

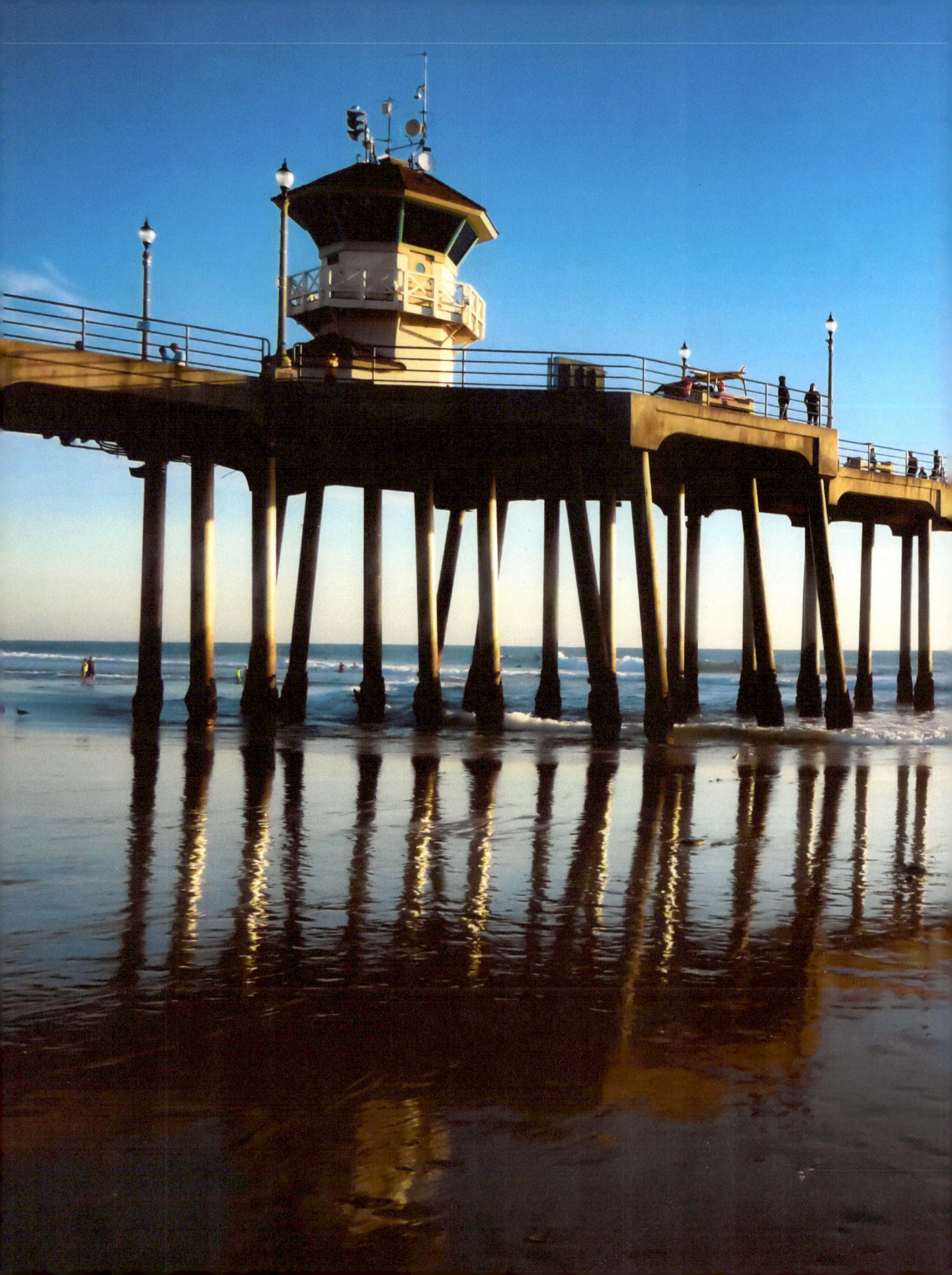

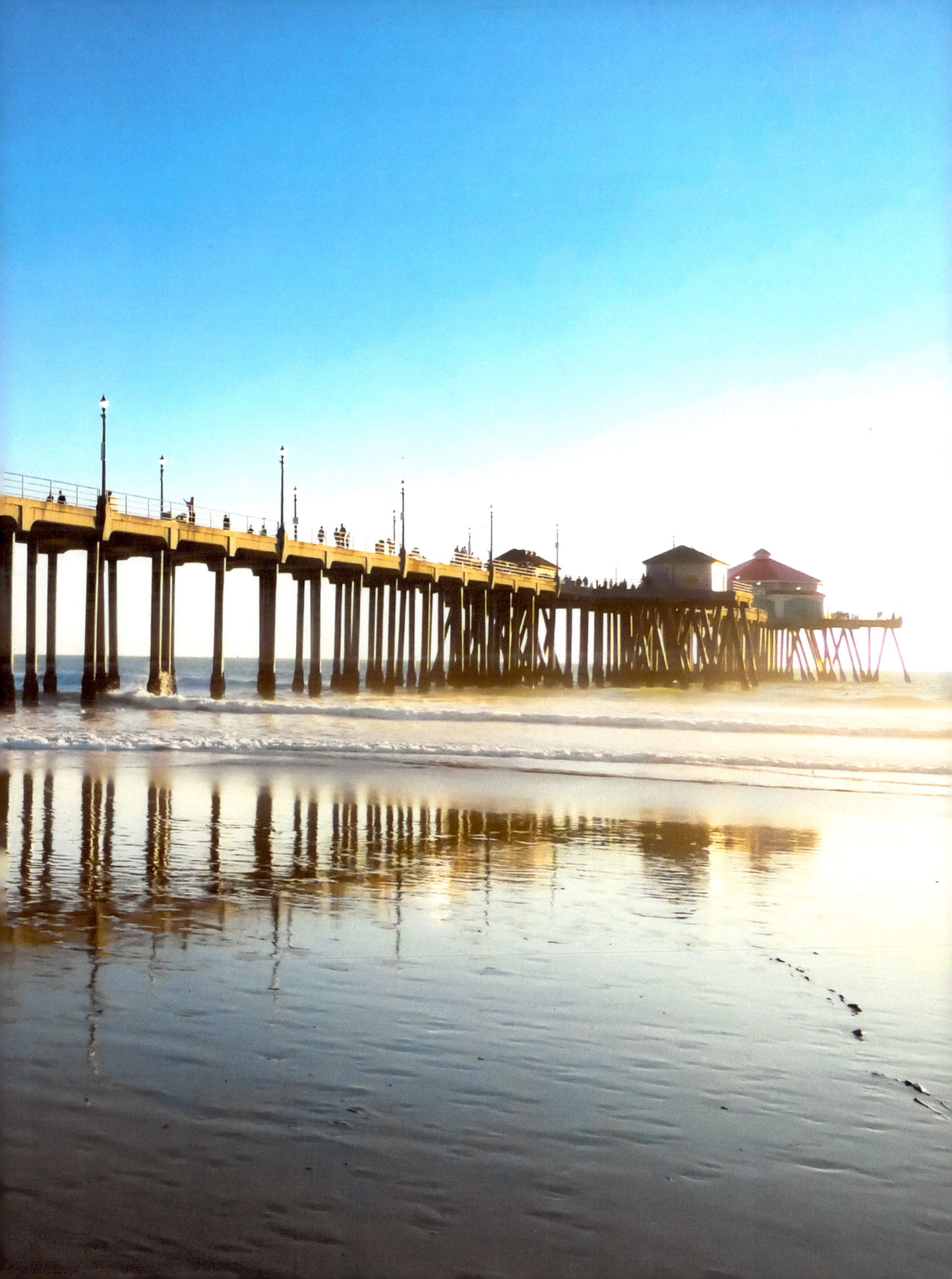

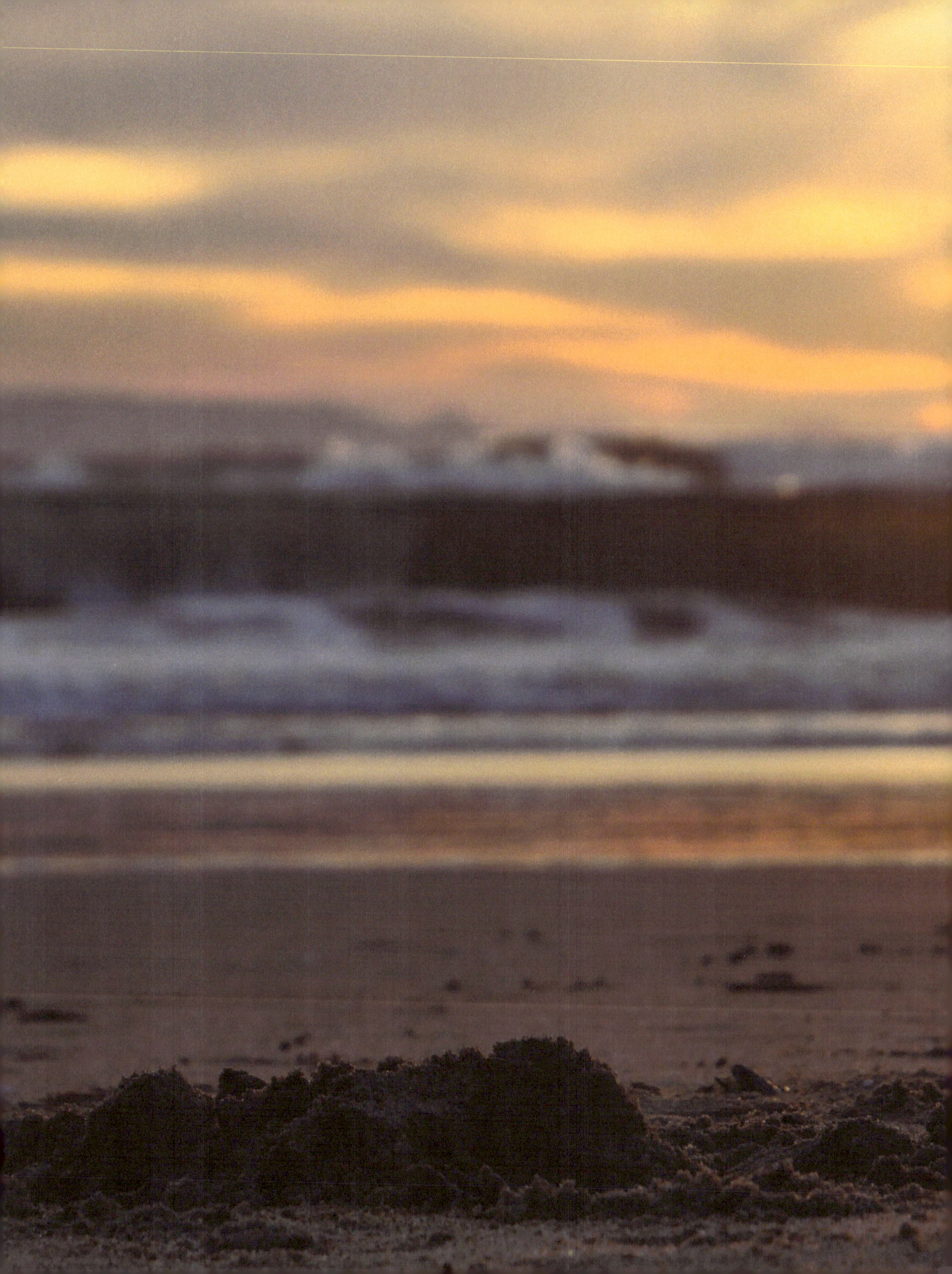

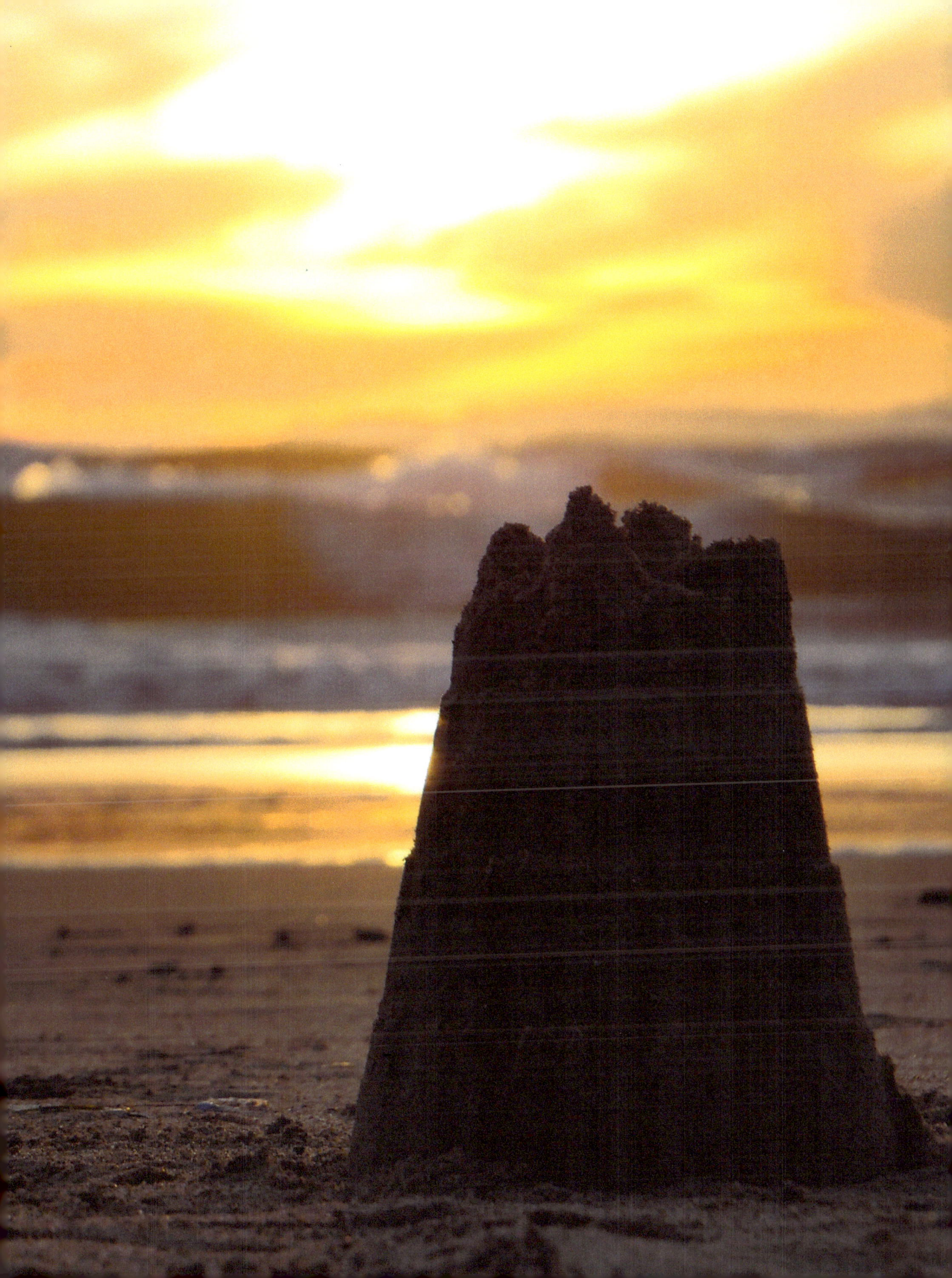

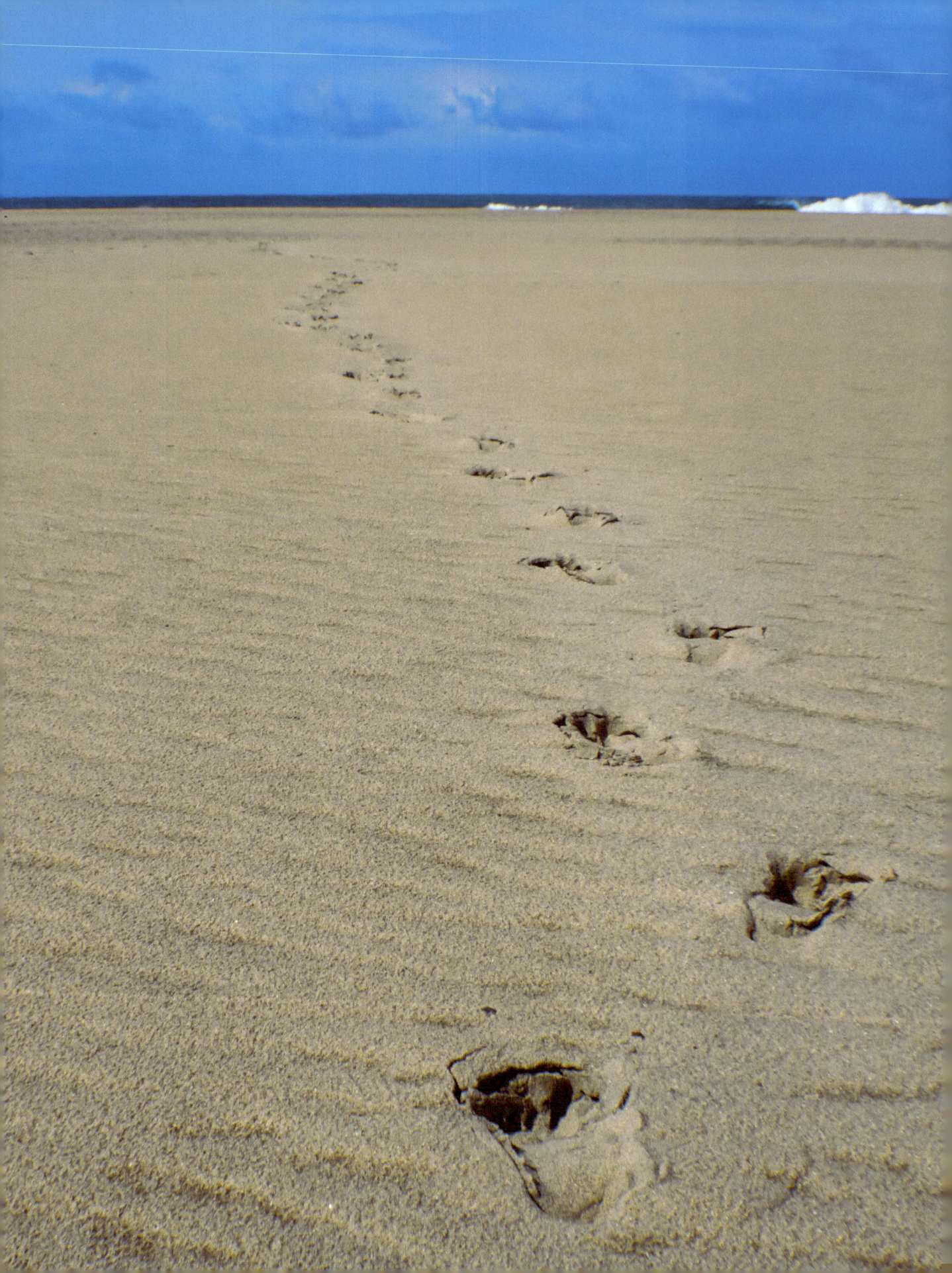

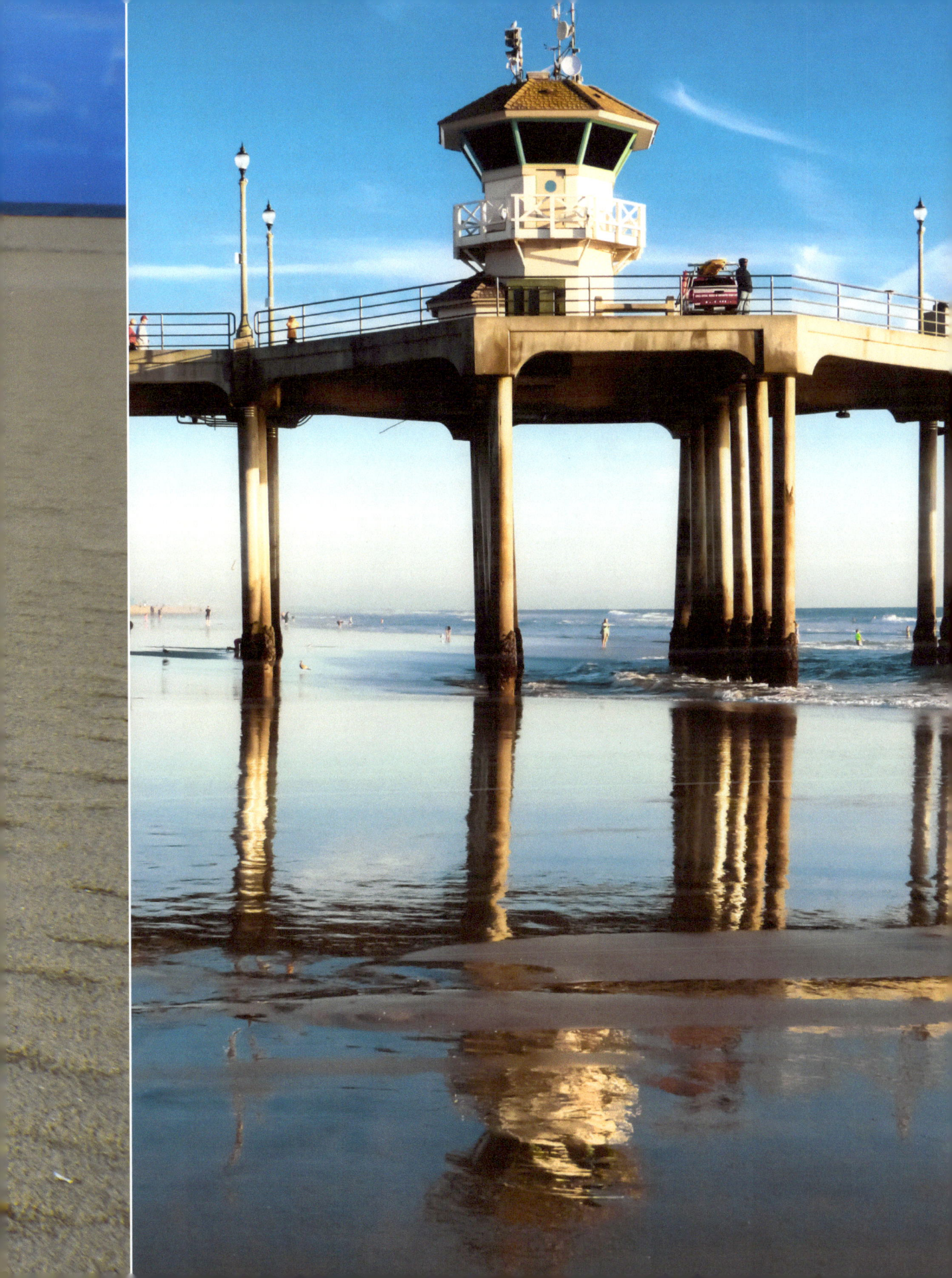

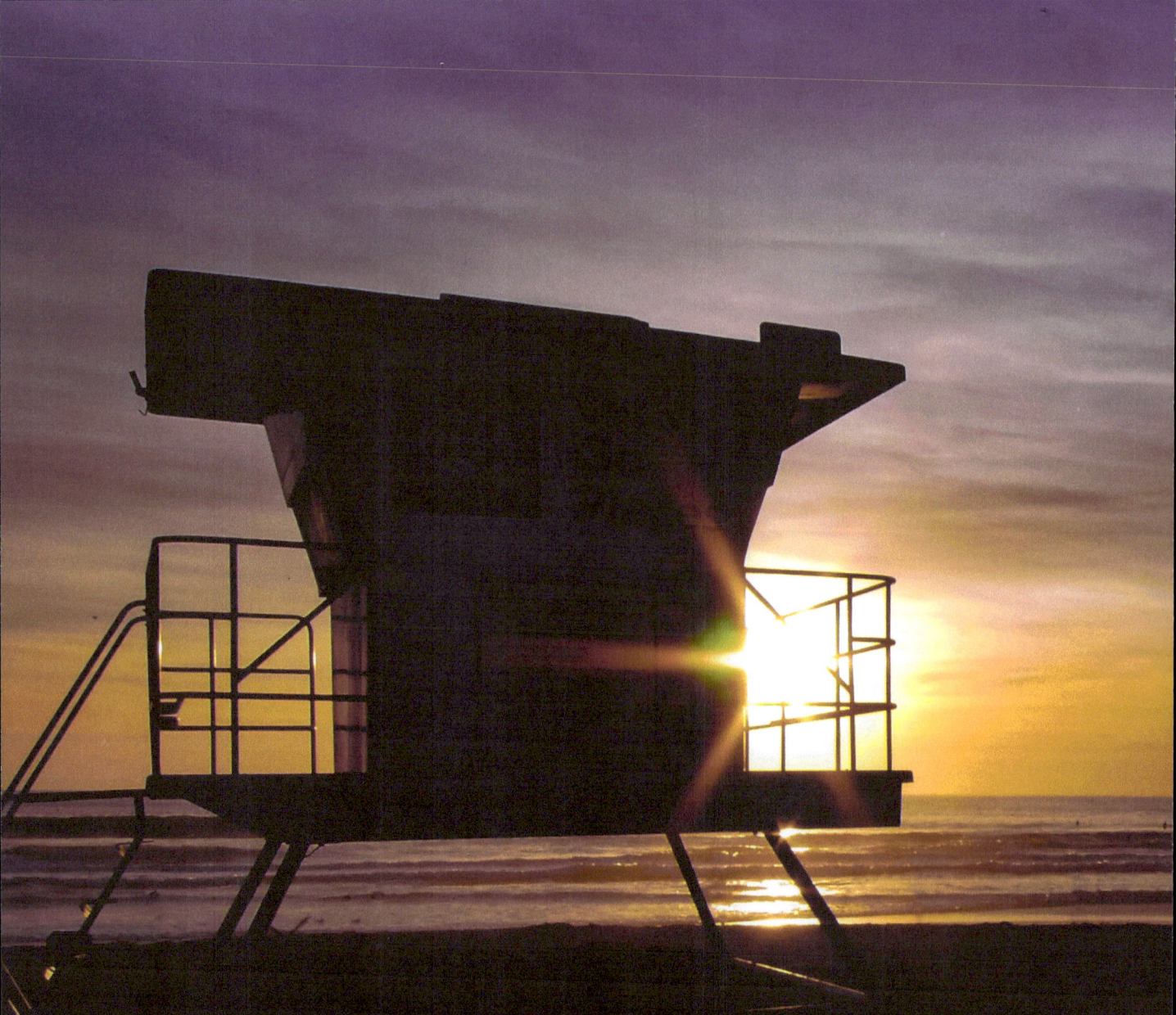

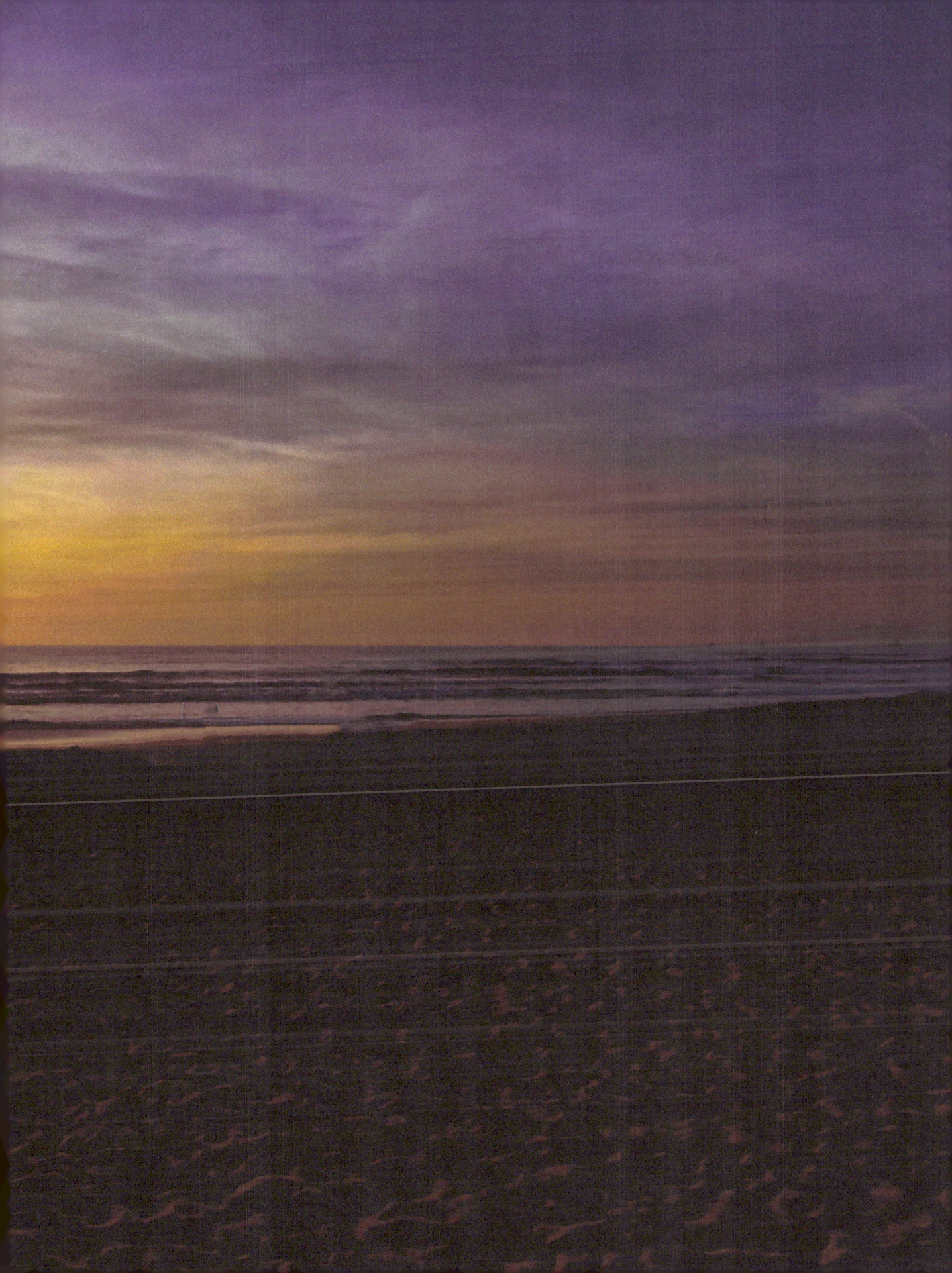

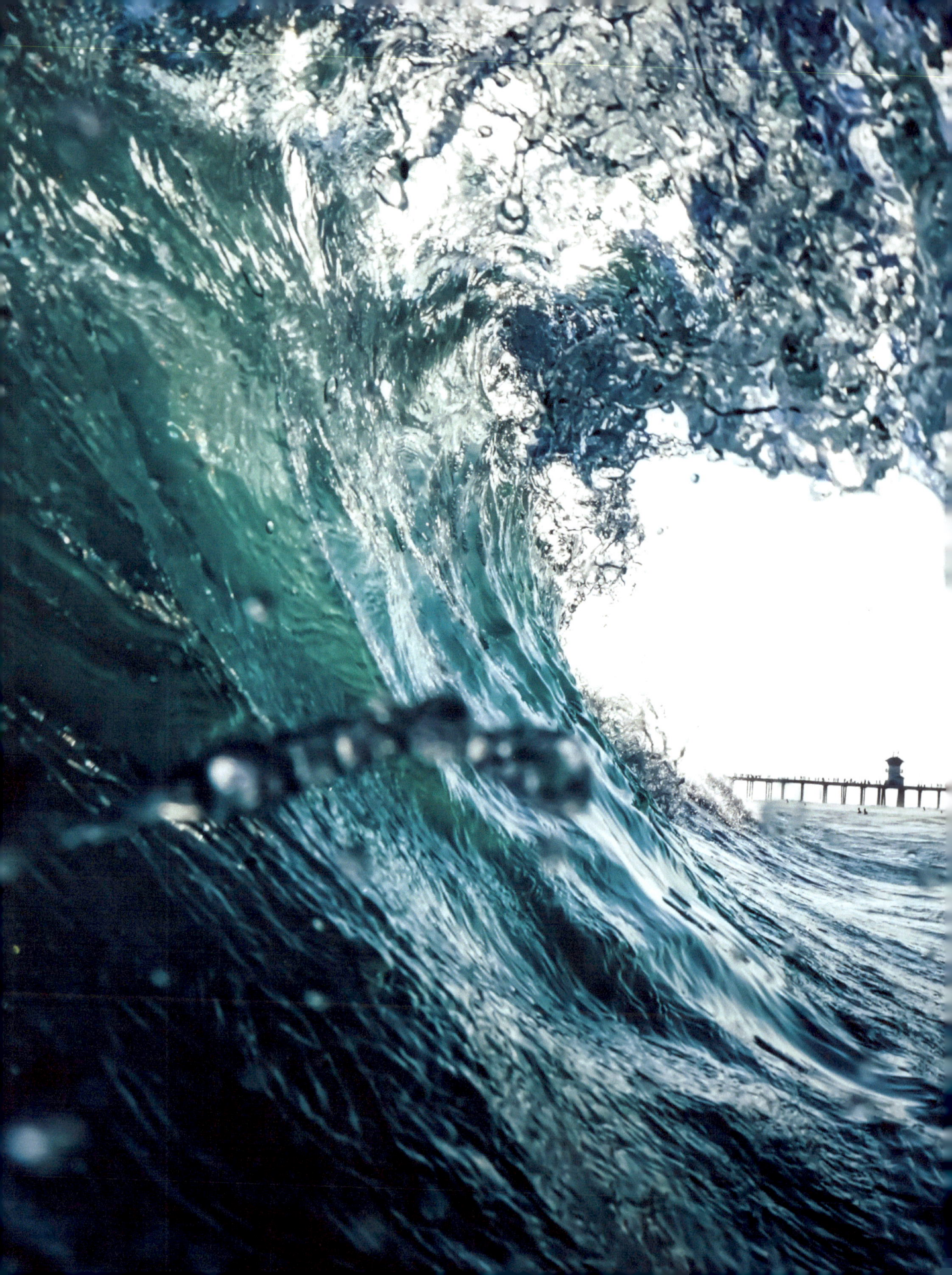

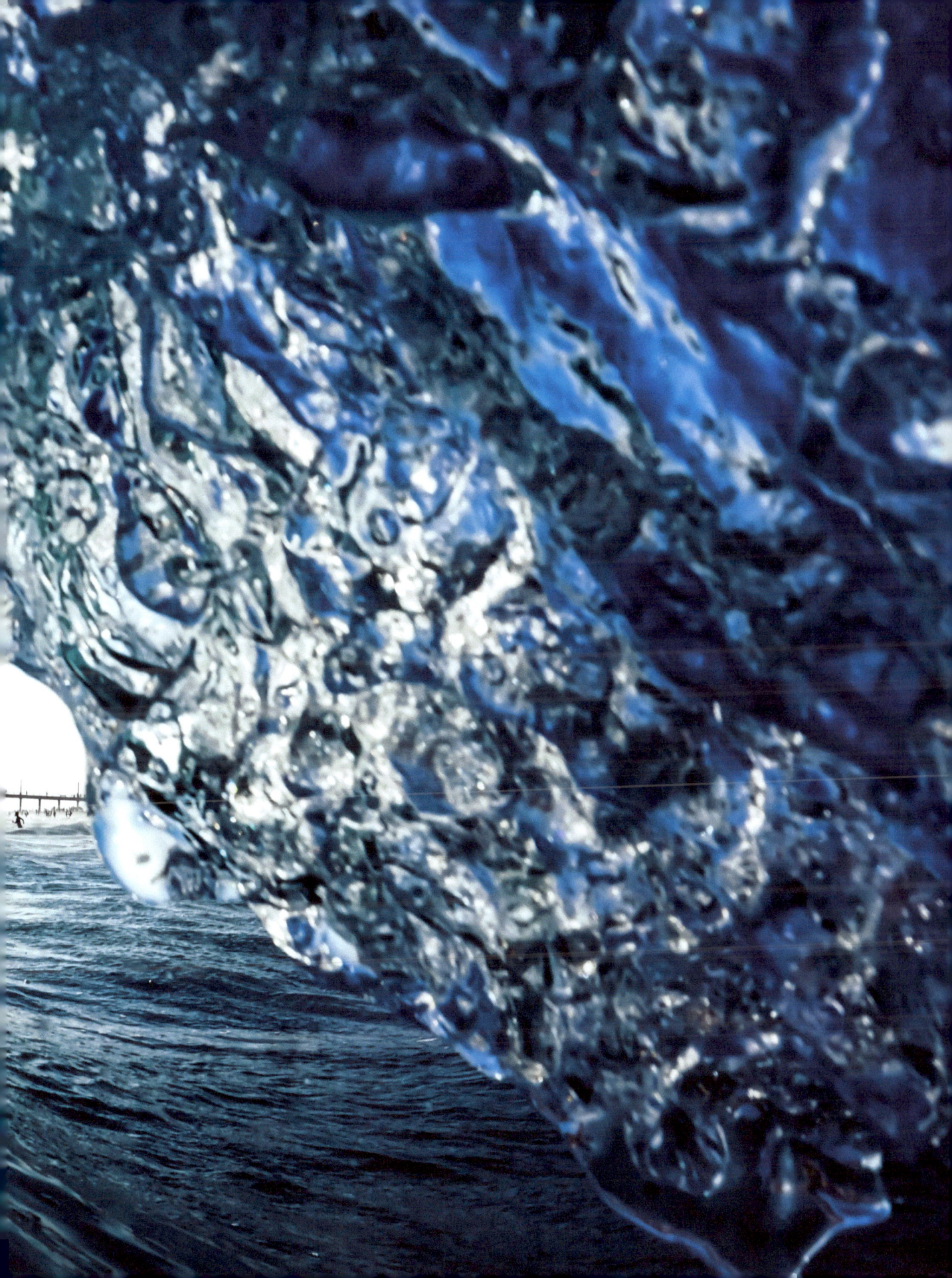

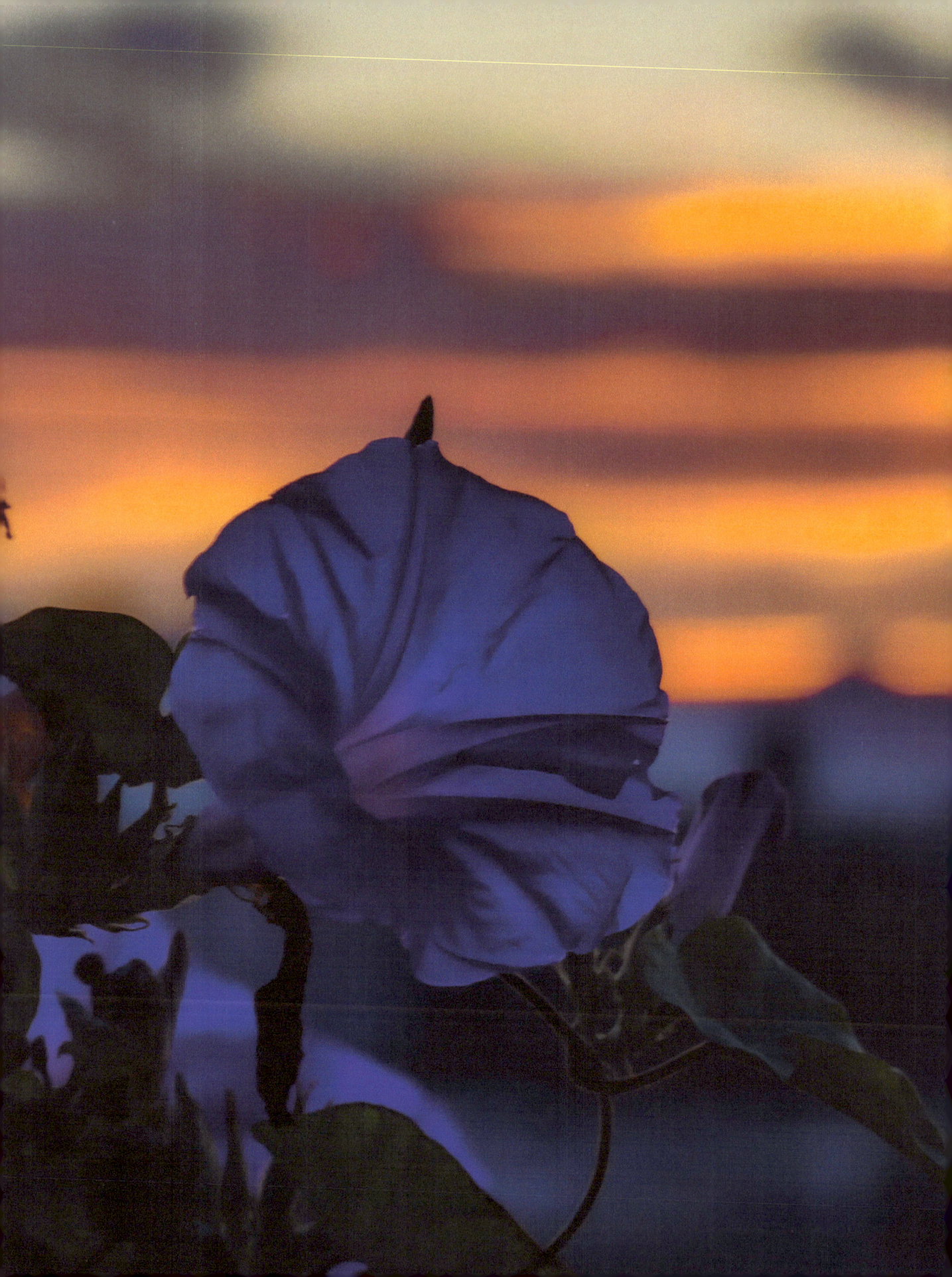

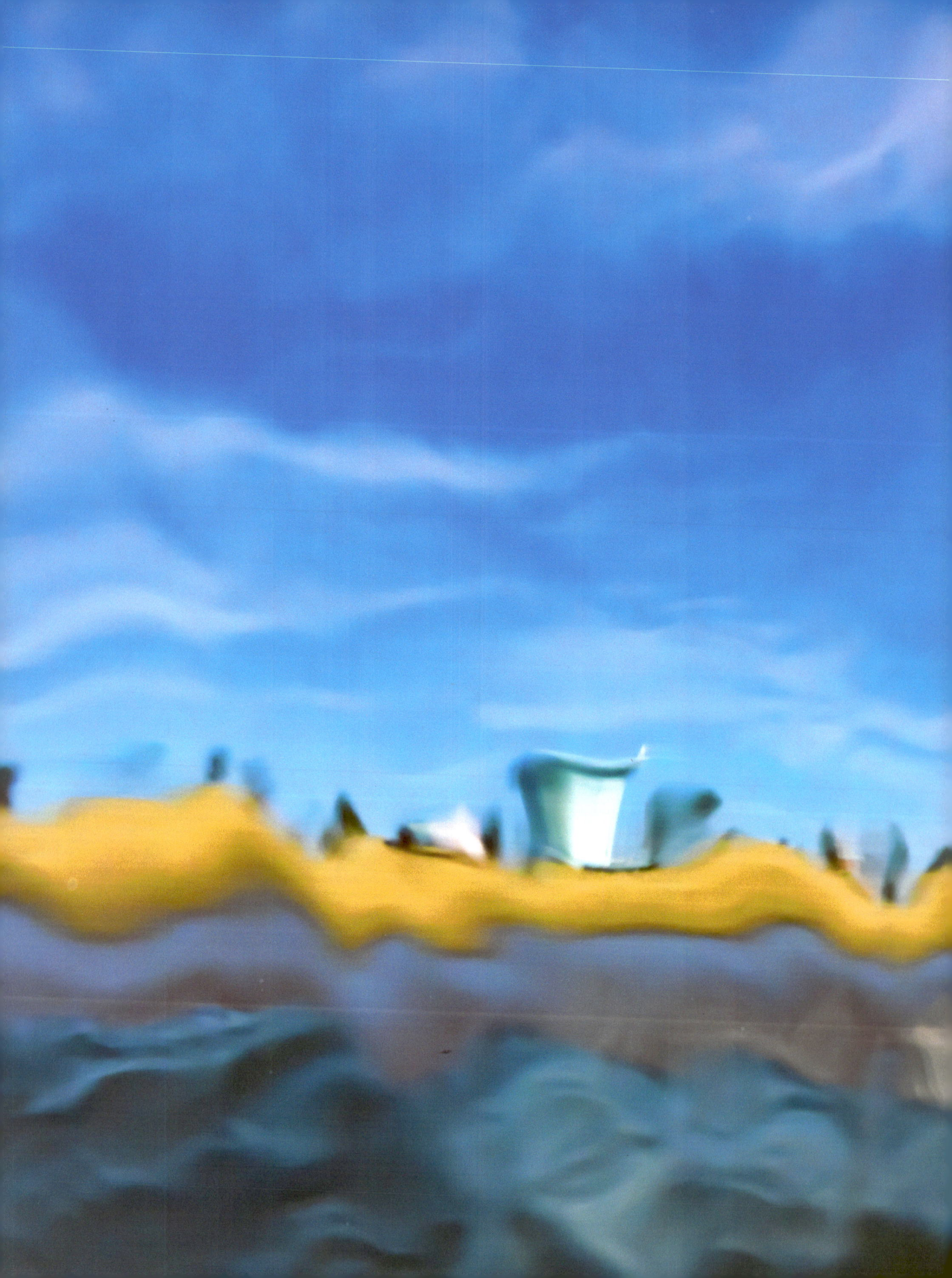

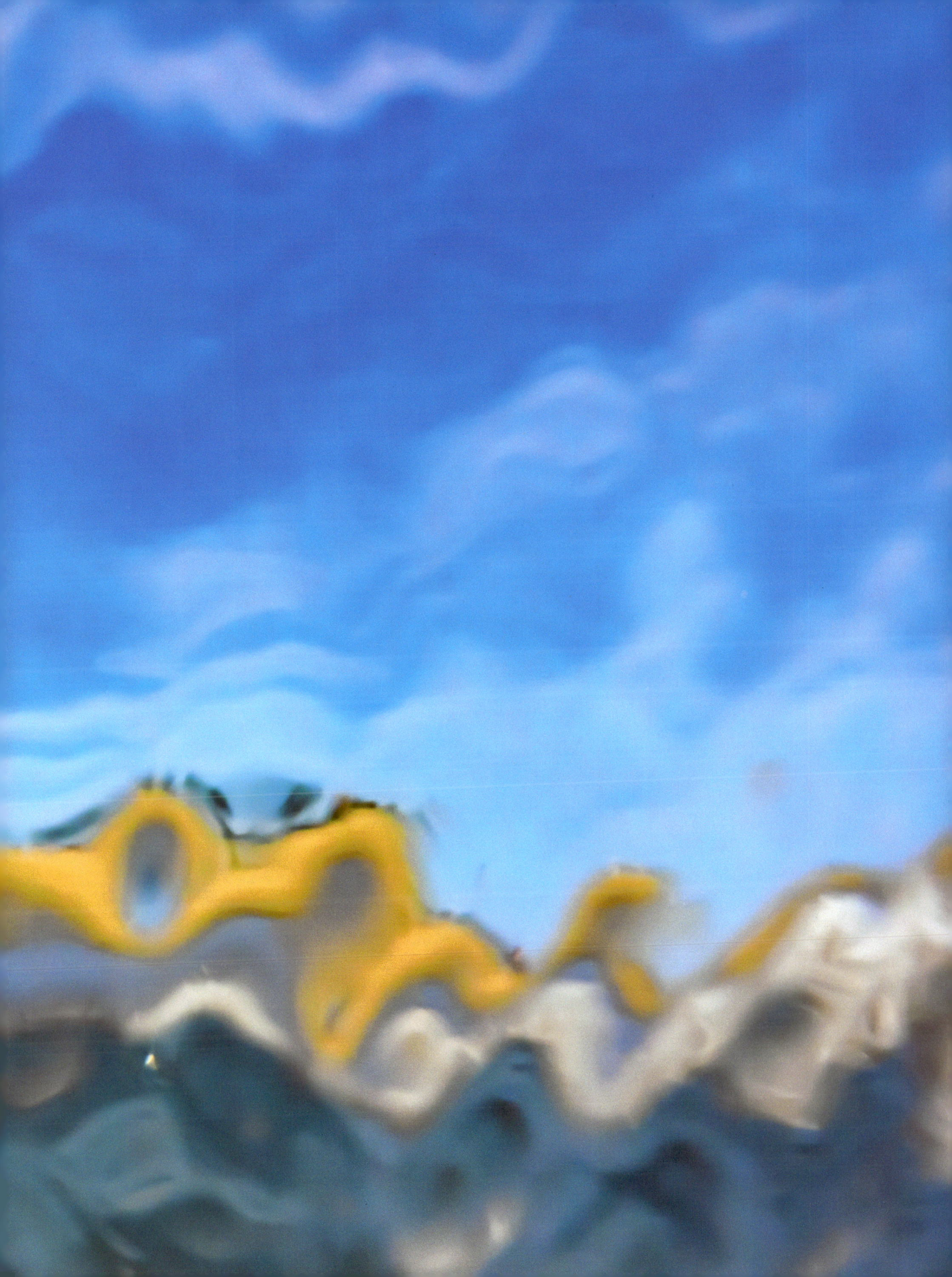

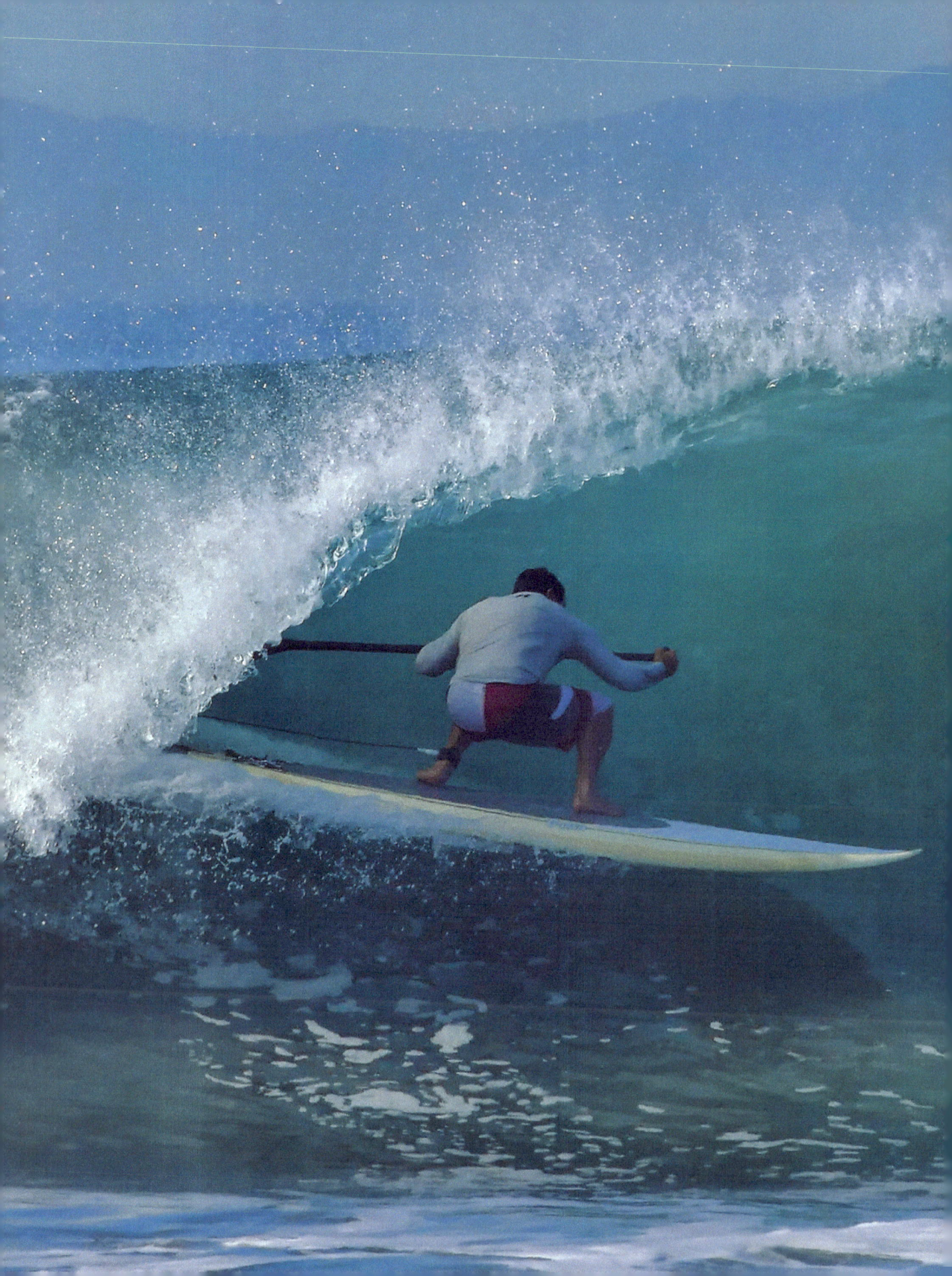

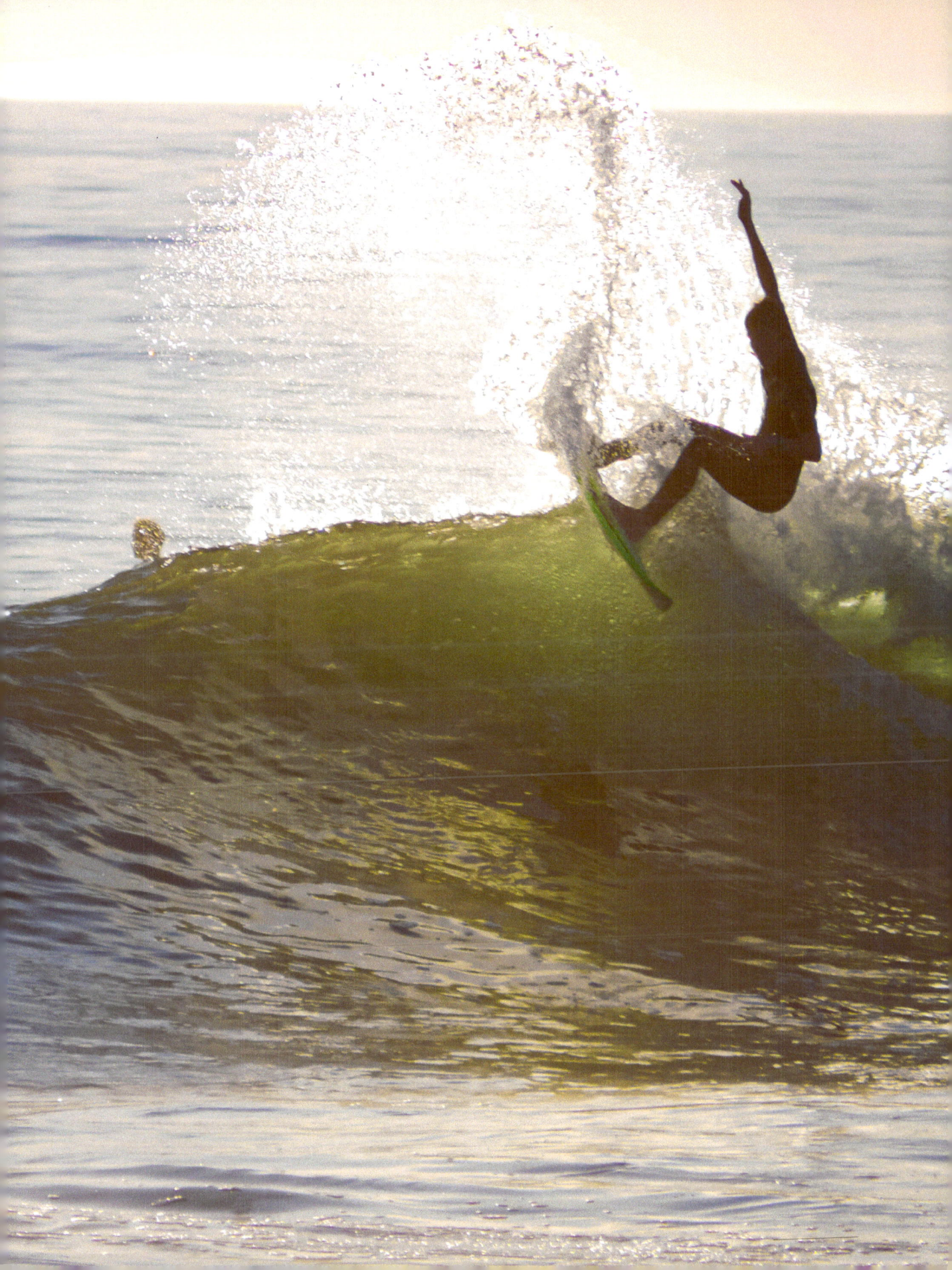

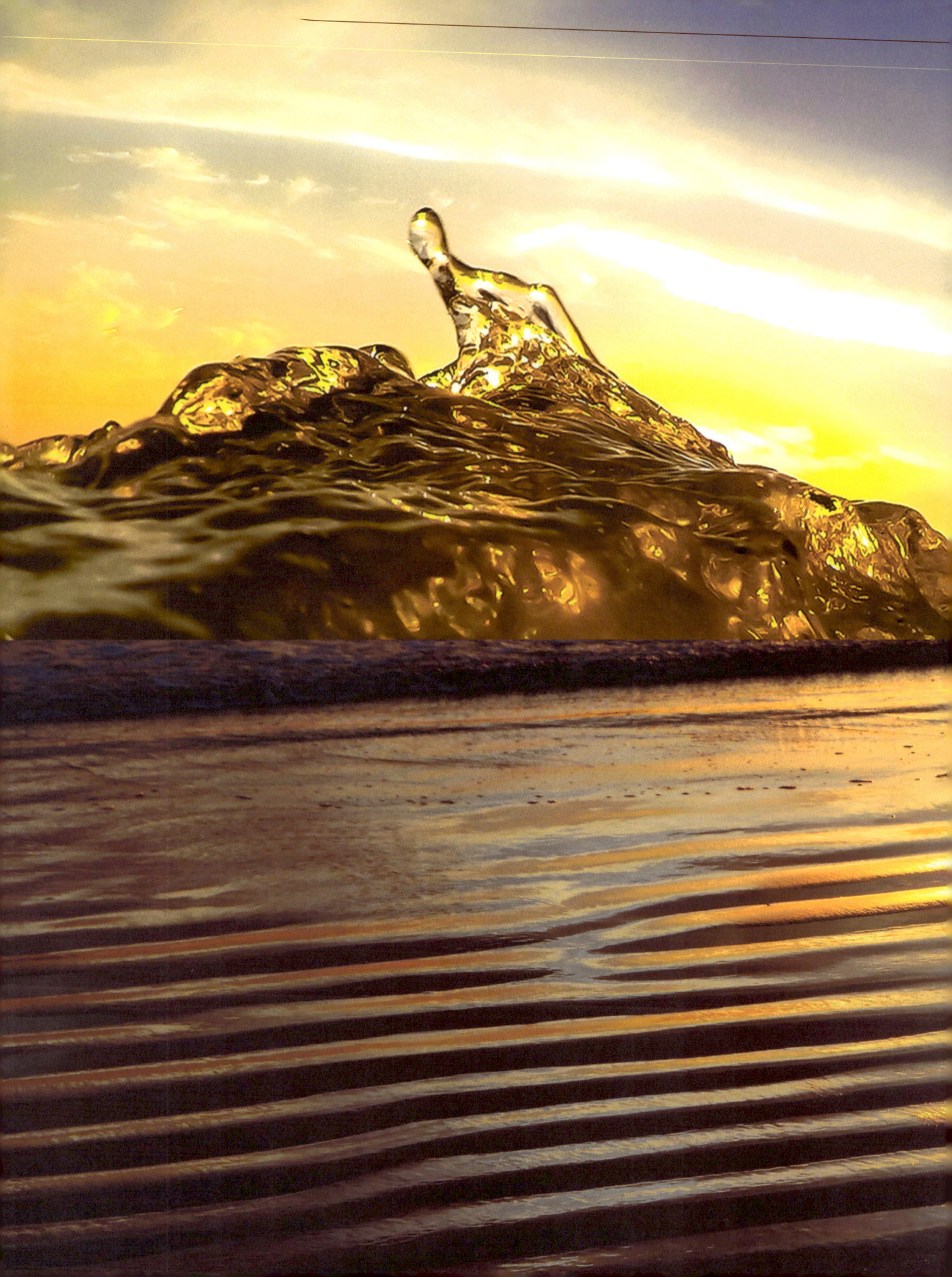

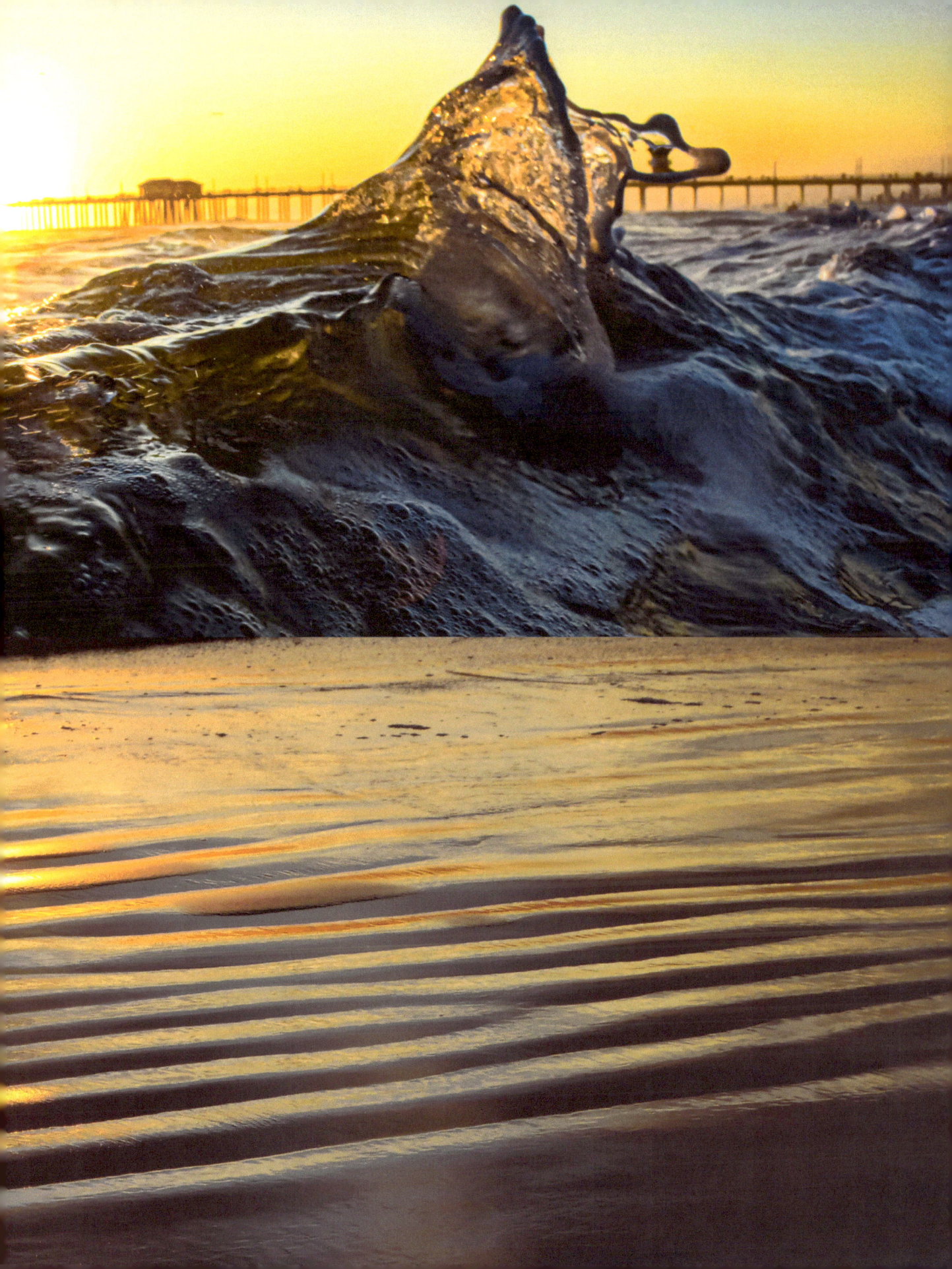

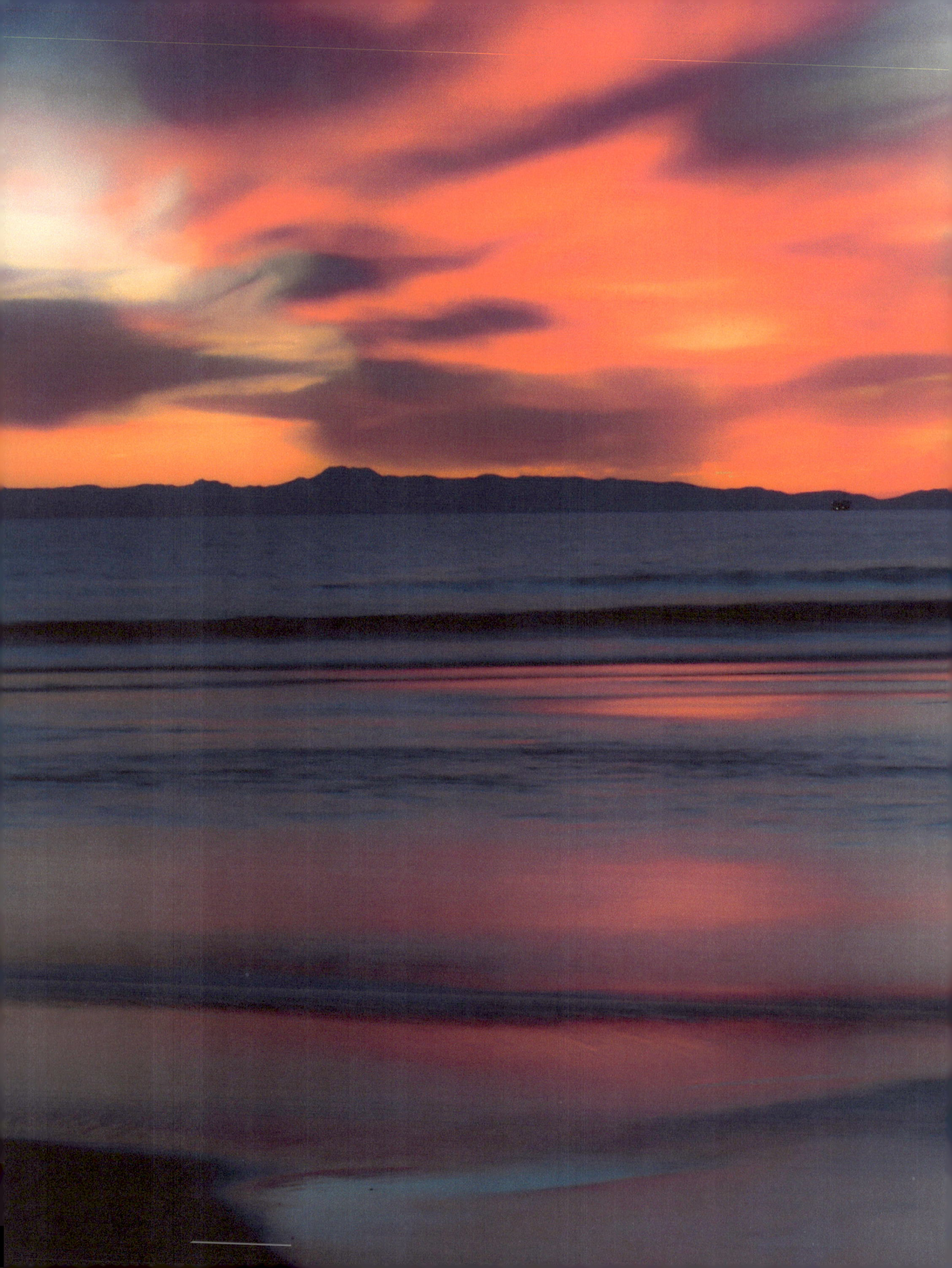

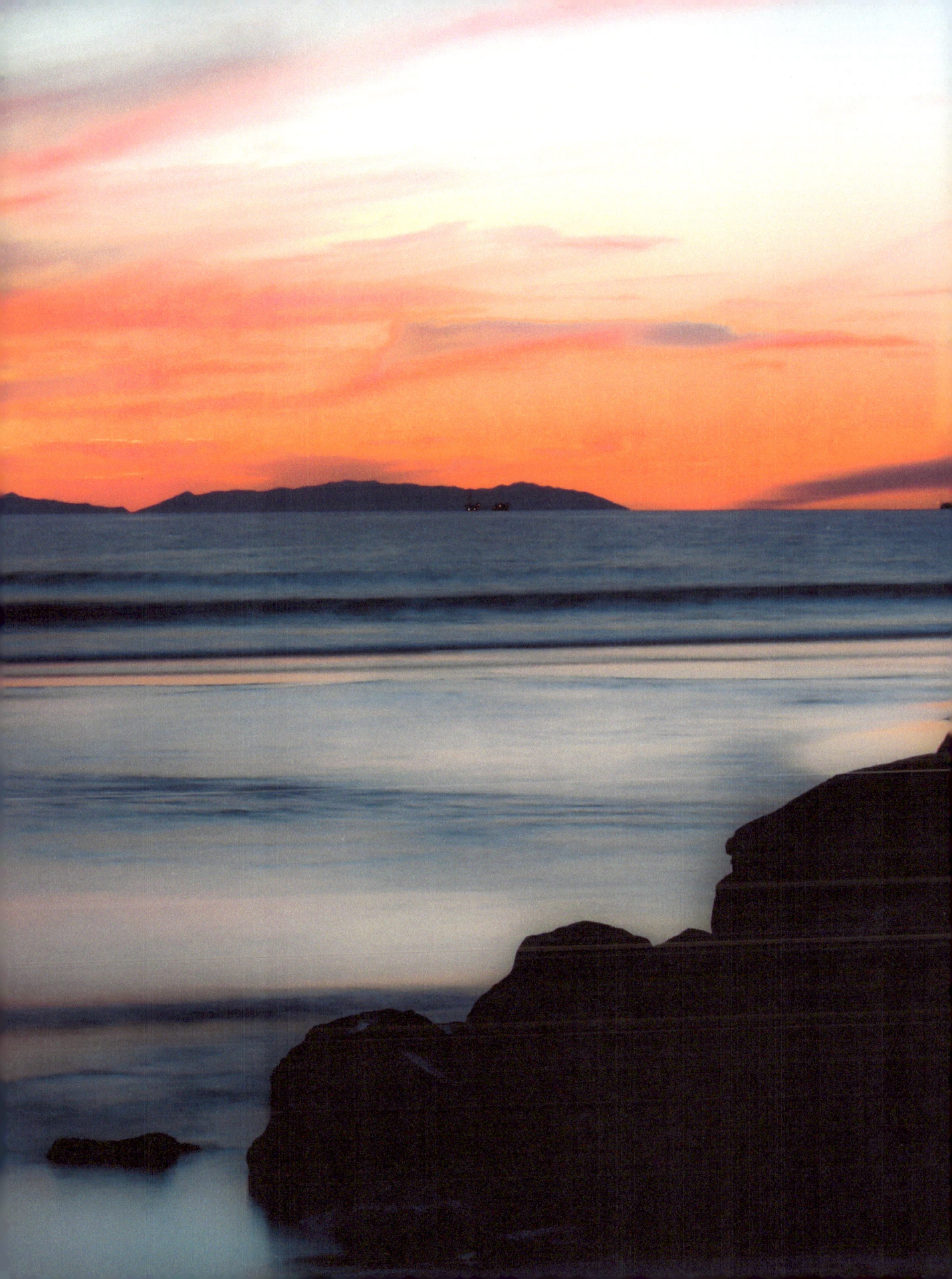

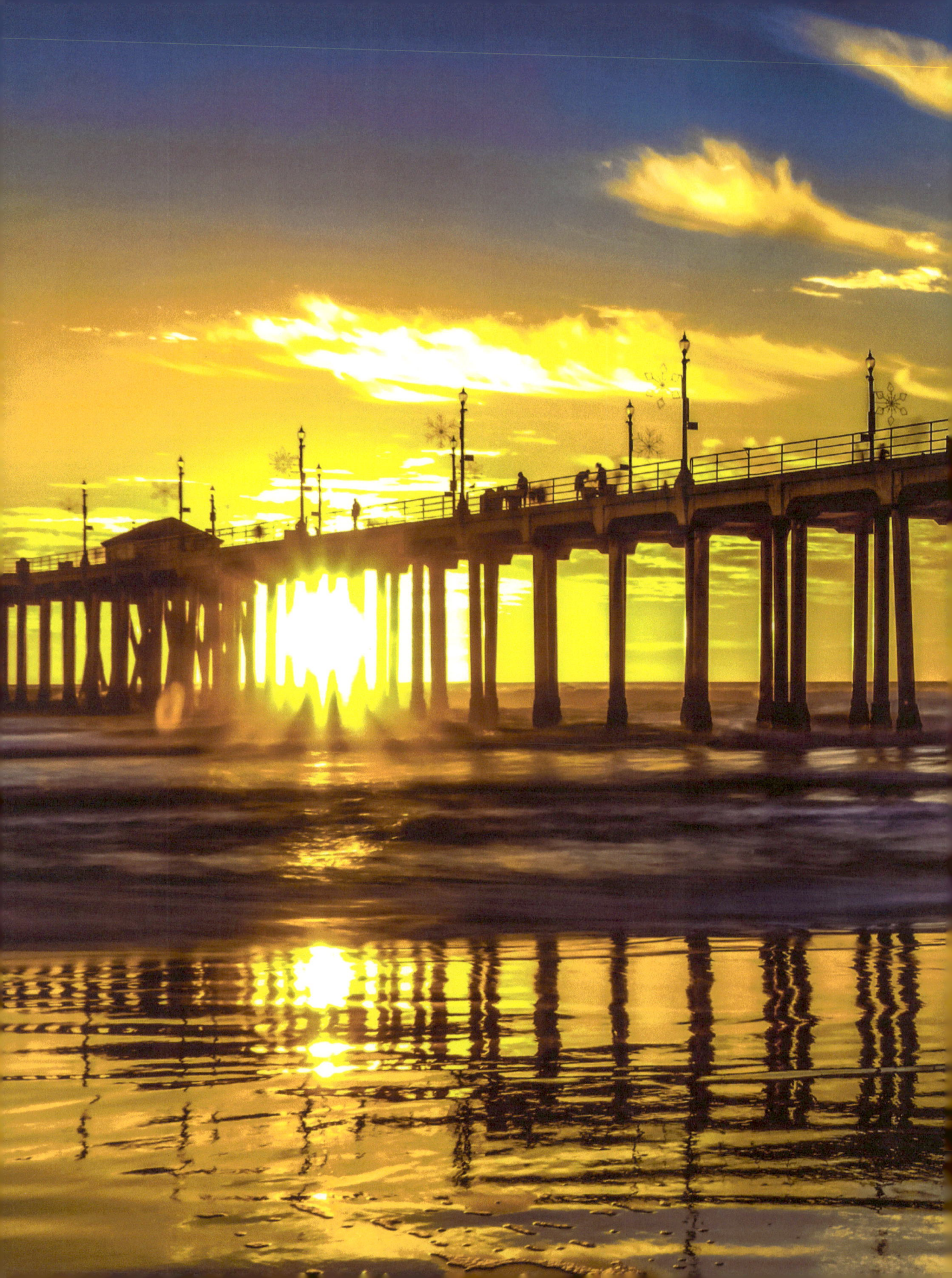

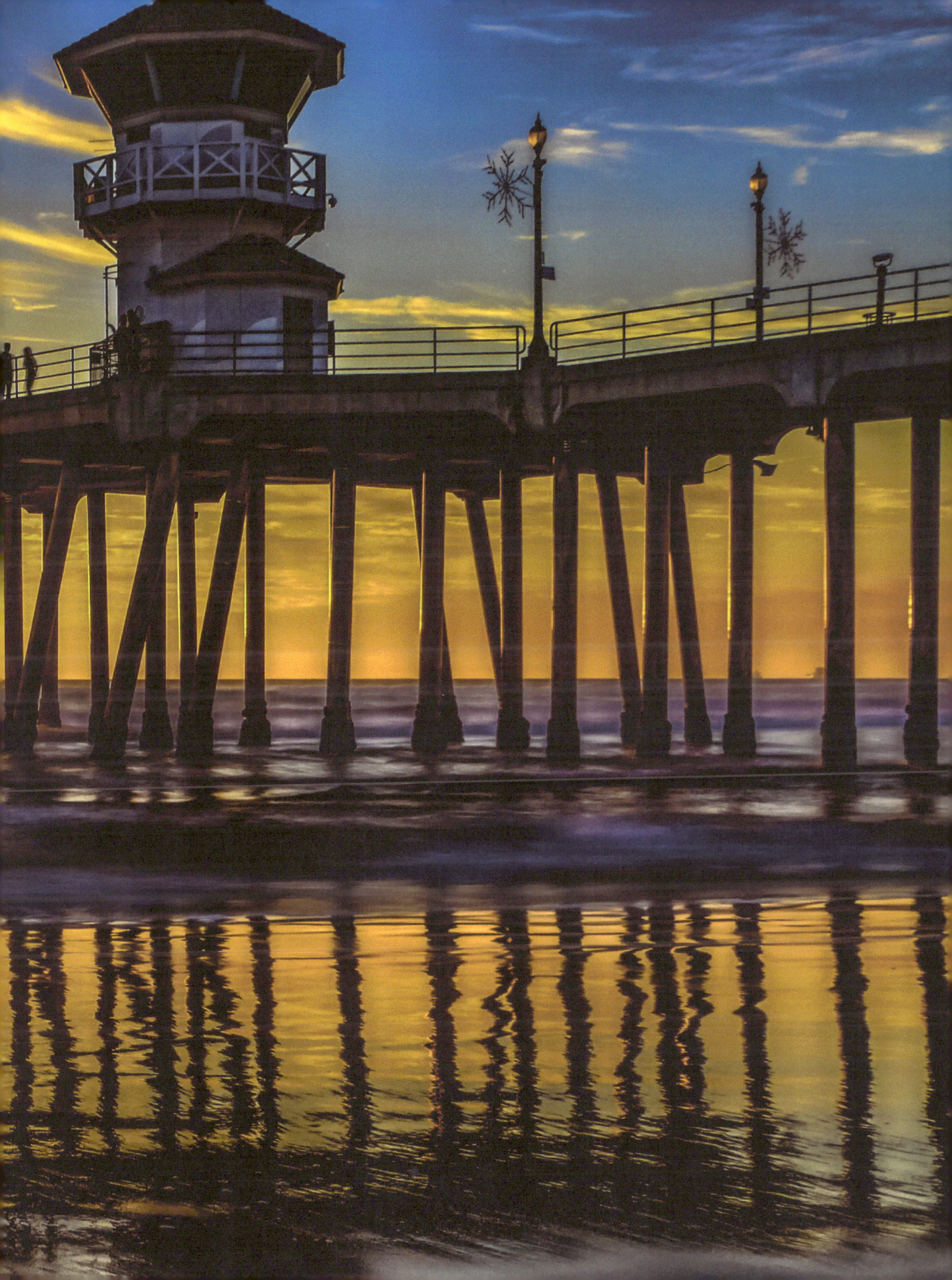

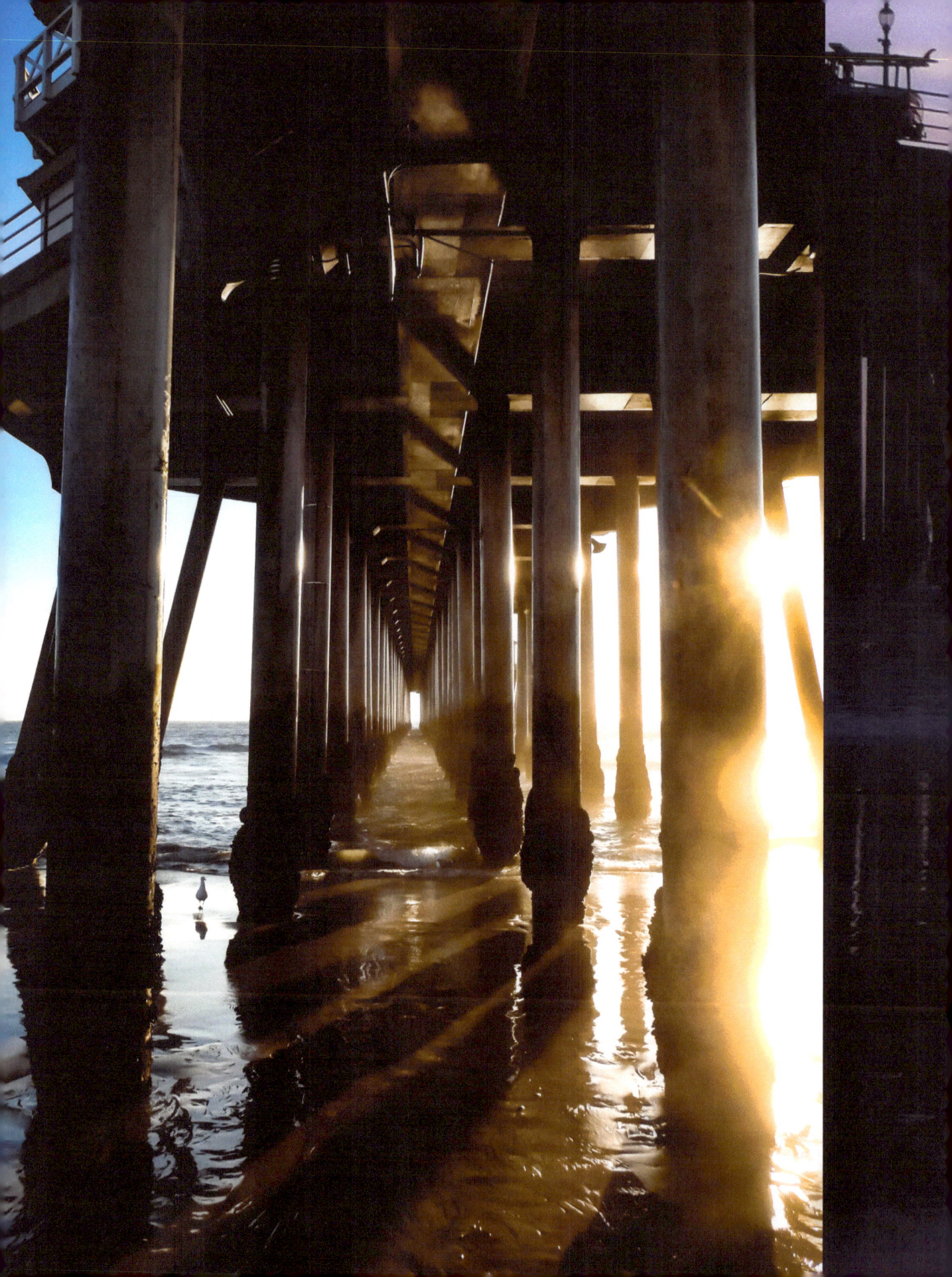

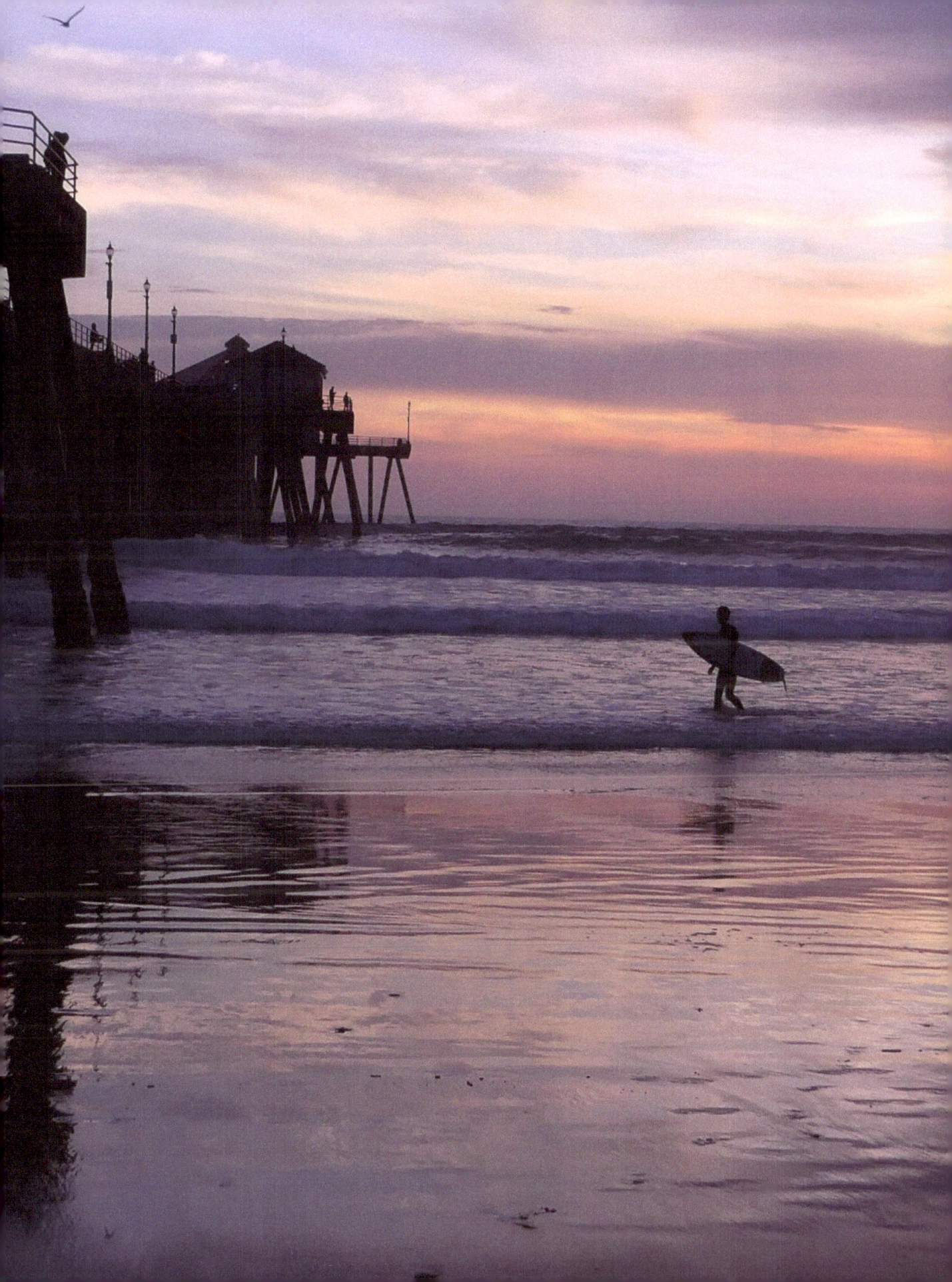

PHOTO LEGEND

1. **Twin Suns**: Huntington Beach is known for both its amazing sunsets and surfing. I attempt to combine the two whenever possible. Ryan Creasey and Issac Durand were kind enough to lend their modeling talents for this HB reflection.
2. **Iconic Reflection**: One of the most iconic and memorable details of Huntington Beach is its pier. From the pier, visitors can see picturesque views of the ocean, the City, and the coastline.
3. **My Kingdom for a Sandcastle**: The high tide was rolling in and slowly washing away the artistry of a beach goer. This photo captures the final remnants of the castle and the sunset.
4. **Footprints**: One must get up early to grace the sand with the first set of footprints. In a way, this is a self-portrait. I made the tracks, then circled back around for the photo!
5. **Reflections**: This is the photo that inspired this collection. I have taken hundreds, if not thousands of pictures of the Huntington Beach pier and the lifeguard tower, but this one brought everything together at just the right moment, including this perfect reflection.
6. **Tower 4**: The color on any given night in Huntington Beach is amazing. The sunset may start as something yellow and orange and transition through red and pink, before settling on a purple hue. This picture gives a since of the variety in one night as purple turns to orange in the fading light.
7. **Friday Afternoon**: A little luck, timing, and know-how, brought this photo together. It's a rewarding feeling when you find and photograph a barrel with a subject perfectly framed on the other side.
8. **Secret Spot**: While the sunsets are amazing in Huntington Beach, the sunrises can be equally enticing, if you know where to go. This is my secret spot for sunrises.
9. **Watercolor**: Wait a minute! This is a photograph. As I rose from the surf, the water dripped over the lens distorting the image to create this wonderful watercolor-like photo.
10. **In Search Of (Paddleboarder and Surfer)**: Huntington Beach may be best known for its surfers, such as the person pictured on the right hitting the lip of the wave, but in this instance on the left, a paddleboarder chases the perfect wave on a fall morning.
11. **The Shape of Water**: The three photos in this spread (Golden Hue, Seahorse, Textures) capture the water during some beautiful moments and sunsets.
12. **Soft Touch**: When people see this picture, I am often asked what I did to it in post-processing. The answer is simple. Nothing. This is untouched and out of the camera with a very long, slow shutter creating the smoothness of the water and a gorgeous sunset providing the natural color.
13. **Sunset on the Southside**: Color, reflections, structure, and nature come together to capture the beauty of Huntington Beach.
14. **Obligatory**: Whether you are a seasoned pro or a casual snapper, every photographer who visits the pier wants to get the photo from below. Here's one that captures the majesty of the pier and the sun. One of my personal favorites.
15. **Purple Surf**: A sunset glowing with purple always amazes, seeming simultaneously unnatural and beautiful. In this photo, a surfer ends his session in the purple hues of the setting sun.
16. **Front Cover:** Another of my personal favorites. This pic was taken from in the waer with a breaking wave to the left and the pier on the horizon with the setting sun just beyond.
17. **Back Cover:** Another majestic HB sunset, filled with textures and color. Fortunate timing.